Hidden AI Guide for Beginners

Contents

Introduction to artificial intelligence (AI)

Artificial intelligence applications are all around us, but what does it really mean? In this article, Kumar Abhishek explains the history and progress of artificial intelligence.

Artificial intelligence (AI) is the ability of machines to replicate or enhance human intellect, such as reasoning and learning from experience. Artificial intelligence has been used in computer programs for years, but it is now applied to many other products and services. For example, some digital cameras can determine what objects are present in an image using artificial intelligence software. In addition, experts predict many more innovative uses for artificial intelligence in the future, including smart electric grids.

AI uses techniques from probability theory, economics, and algorithm design to solve practical problems. In addition, the AI field draws upon computer science, mathematics, psychology, and linguistics. Computer science provides tools for designing and building algorithms, while mathematics offers tools for modeling and solving the resulting optimization problems.

Although the concept of AI has been around since the 19th century, when Alan Turing first proposed an "imitation game" to assess machine intelligence, it only became feasible to achieve in recent decades due to the increased availability of computing power and data to train AI systems.

To understand the idea behind AI, you should think about what distinguishes human intelligence from that of other creatures – our ability to learn from experiences and apply these lessons to new situations. We can do this because of our advanced brainpower; we have more neurons than any animal species.

Today's computers don't match the human biological neural network – not even close. But they have one significant advantage over us: their ability to analyze vast amounts of data and experiences much faster than humans could ever hope.

AI lets you focus on the most critical tasks and make better decisions based on acquired data related to a use case. It can be used for complex tasks, such as predicting maintenance requirements, detecting credit card fraud, and finding the best route for a delivery truck. In other words, AI can automate many business processes leaving you to concentrate on your core business.

Research in the field is concerned with producing machines to automate tasks requiring intelligent behavior. Examples include control, planning and scheduling, the ability to answer diagnostic and consumer questions, handwriting, natural language processing and perception, speech recognition, and the ability to move and manipulate objects.

History of AI and how it has progressed over the years

With so much attention on modern artificial intelligence, it is easy to forget that the field is not brand new. AI has had a number of different periods, distinguished by whether the focus was on proving logical theorems or trying to mimic human thought via neurology.

Artificial intelligence dates back to the late 1940s when computer pioneers like Alan Turing and John von Neumann first started examining how machines could "think." However, a significant milestone in AI occurred in 1956 when researchers proved that a machine could solve any problem if it were allowed to use an unlimited amount of memory. The result was a program called the General Problem Solver (GPS).

Over the next two decades, research efforts focused on applying artificial intelligence to real-world problems. This development led to expert systems, which allow machines to learn from experience and make predictions based on gathered data. Expert systems aren't as complex as human brains, but they can be trained to identify patterns and make decisions based on that data. They're commonly used in medicine and manufacturing today.

A second major milestone came in 1965 with the development of programs like Shakey the robot and ELIZA, which automated simple conversations between humans and machines. These early programs paved the way for more advanced speech recognition technology, eventually leading to Siri and Alexa.

The initial surge of excitement around artificial intelligence lasted about ten years. It led to significant advances in programming language design, theorem proving, and robotics. But it also provoked a backlash against over-hyped claims that had been made for the field, and funding was cut back sharply around 1974.

After a decade without much progress, interest revived in the late 1980s. This revival was primarily driven by reports that machines were becoming better than humans at "narrow" tasks like playing checkers or chess and advances in computer vision and speech recognition. This time, the emphasis was on building systems that could understand and learn from real-world data with less human intervention.

These developments continued slowly until 1992, when interest began to increase again. First, technological advances in computing power and information storage helped boost interest in research on artificial intelligence. Then, in the mid-1990s, another major boom was driven by considerable advances in computer hardware that had taken place since the early 1980s. The result has been dramatic improvements in performance on several significant benchmark problems, such as image recognition, where machines are now almost as good as humans at some tasks.

The early years of the 21st century were a period of significant progress in artificial intelligence. The first major advance was the development of the self-learning neural network. By 2001, its performance had already surpassed human beings in many specific areas, such as object classification and machine translation. Over the next few years, researchers improved its performance across a range of tasks, thanks to improvements in the underlying technologies.

The second significant advancement in this period was the development of generative model-based reinforcement learning algorithms. Generative models can generate novel examples from a given class, which helps learn complex behaviors from very little data. For example, they can be used to learn how to control a car from only 20 minutes of driving experience.

In addition to these two advances, there have been several other significant developments in AI over the past decade. There has been an increasing emphasis on using deep neural networks for computer vision tasks, such as object recognition and scene understanding. There has also been an increased focus on using machine learning tools for natural language processing tasks such as information extraction and question answering. Finally, there has been a growing interest in using these same tools for speech recognition tasks like automatic speech recognition (ASR) and speaker identification (SID).

Different fields under AI to clear common misconceptions

Artificial Intelligence is the most trending field of computer science. However, with all the new technology and research, it's growing so fast that it can be confusing to understand what is what. Furthermore, there are many different fields within AI, each one having its specific algorithms. Therefore, it's essential to know that AI is not a single field but a combination of various fields.

Artificial Intelligence (AI) is the general term for being able to make computers do things that require intelligence if done by humans. AI can be broken down into two major fields, Machine Learning (ML) and Neural Networks (NN). Both are subfields under Artificial Intelligence, and each one has its methods and algorithms to help solve problems.

- Artificial intelligence
- machine learning
- Deep learning

Machine learning

Machine Learning (ML) makes computers learn from data and experience to improve their performance on some tasks or decision-making processes. ML uses statistics and probability theory for this purpose. Machine learning uses algorithms to parse data, learn from it, and make determinations without explicit programming. Machine learning algorithms are often categorized as supervised or unsupervised. Supervised algorithms can apply what has been learned in the past to new data sets; unsupervised algorithms can draw inferences from datasets. Machine learning algorithms are designed to strive to establish linear and non-linear relationships in a given set of data. This feat is achieved by statistical methods used to train the algorithm to classify or predict from a dataset.

Deep learning

Deep learning is a subset of machine learning that uses multi-layered artificial neural networks to deliver state-of-the-art accuracy in object detection, speech recognition and language translation. Deep learning is a crucial technology behind driverless cars and enables the machine analysis of large amounts of complex data — for example, recognizing the faces of people who appear in an image or video.

Neural networks

Neural networks are inspired by biological neurons in the human brain and are composed of layers of connected nodes called "neurons" that contain mathematical functions to process incoming data and predict an output value. Artificial neural network learns by example, similarly to how humans learn from our parents, teachers, and peers. They consist of at least three layers: an input layer, hidden layers, and an output layer. Each layer contains nodes (also known as neurons) which have weighted inputs that compute the output.

The performance of traditional machine learning models plateau and throwing any more data doesn't help improve the performance. Deep learning models continue to improve in performance with more data.

These fields have different algorithms, depending on the use case. For example, we have decision trees, random forests, boosting, support vector machines (SVM), k-nearest neighbors (kNN), and others for machine learning. For neural networks, we have convolutional neural networks (CNNs), recurrent neural networks (RNNs), long short-term memory networks (LSTMs), and more.

However, classifying AI according to its strength and capabilities would mean further subdividing it into "narrow AI" and "general AI." Narrow AI is about getting machines to do one task really well, like image recognition or playing chess. General AI means devices that can do everything humans can do and more. Today's research focuses on narrow AI, but many researchers would like machine learning to eventually achieve general AI.

How AI stands out in different industries.

AI is a booming technology that the global community has accepted. It has been revolutionizing the industry from various sectors for quite some time. It is a comprehensive technology that is being applied in almost every industry. This section discusses how AI is impacting service delivery in various sectors.

Fully self-driving cars are now a reality. Tesla is the first company to make a car with all of the sensors, cameras, and software needed for a computer to drive itself from start to finish. Trucks may be the next primary target for autonomy: self-driving trucks will enormously impact road safety and infrastructure and save companies money by reducing labor costs.

A few other industries are also implementing AI. For example, in finance, AI helps with forecasting and supports hedge-fund investment decisions. Predictive analytics (or forecasting) applies artificial intelligence using machine learning and statistical techniques to make predictions about future events based on previous data. For example, you can use forecasting to predict product sales, customer demand, or even stock prices. One popular example of predictive analytics is Amazon's product recommendations engine (also known as "Customers who bought this item also bought"). It uses past purchase data from millions of customers to recommend products based on the users' preferences.

In healthcare, AI is helping doctors to diagnose diseases by gathering data from health records, scanning reports, and medical images. This helps doctors to make faster diagnoses and guide the patient for further tests or prescribe medications. In addition, AI can be used in the treatment process by monitoring patients and alerting their doctors when something goes wrong. According to Forbes, AI will save over 7 million lives in 2035.

In retail, AI does everything from stock management to customer service chatbots. As a result, many businesses are taking advantage of AI to improve productivity, efficiency, and accuracy. In addition, companies find new ways to use AI to make life easier for their customers and employees, from product design to customer service.

The current state of AI-based software systems.

The recent advancements in AI have led to the emergence of a new type of system called Generative Adversarial Networks (GANs), which generate realistic images, text, or audio. Due to their remarkable capabilities, some people are concerned that this technology could replace humans in the future.

GANs are just one example of how AI is changing our lives. This section explores more current AI examples and its applications in software systems such as GPT3, DALL.E, and virtual reality/augmented reality (VR/AR).

AI-based software systems are comprised of many layers such as foundational models, advanced algorithms, and automated reasoning tools. Some of the most popular AI-based systems that use these layers include GPT3, DALL.E, AlphaGo, RoBERTa, and many others.

DALL.E and GPT3 are large-scale models that have achieved remarkable results in computer vision and natural language processing (NLP).

The GPT3 model is an NLP model based on a deep learning algorithm called transformers. It was trained on a corpus of text from Common Crawl and published in 2020. GPT3 uses a large dataset trained in the English language to produce outputs based on the inputted information. The model can be trained to perform any task imaginable, from generating text to solving math problems. Also, we can use GPT3 to generate text, translate between languages, answer questions about images, and more.

The DALL.E model is an image generator based on a deep learning algorithm called variational autoencoders (VAEs). Similarly, DALL.E can be trained using an image dataset to produce images based on the inputted text descriptions. It was trained on datasets such as ImageNet and published in 2021. We can use DALL.E to generate images that match captions or URLs given by users. These models have been developed by OpenAI, which has close ties to the US government and military-industrial complex (MIC).

DeepMind created AlphaGo as a program that would play the ancient game Go without anyone's help. The game is similar to chess but much more complex due to its simple rules and many possible moves per turn. AlphaGo used reinforcement learning to learn how to play the game better over time by playing against itself repeatedly until it mastered every possible situation that could occur in a game of Go with 100% accuracy.

RoBERTa is an algorithm from Facebook AI Research (FAIR) that uses deep learning techniques to solve problems in natural language processing (NLP), such as sentence classification or machine translation.

The Future of AI. What to expect from AI in the next few years or decades

Artificial intelligence has come a long way, but it's about to make a huge leap. Artificial general intelligence (AGI), the kind of AI capable of doing any intellectual task that a human being can do, is still a ways off, but we're already starting to see plenty of progress in other areas of AI. Here's what you can expect soon:

Artificial Intelligence will make more jobs obsolete as it takes over more and more tasks

The reason why is simple: if you can replace one person with an AGI system, you don't need one computer to do the work – you can spread it out across thousands or millions of computers. That's only possible because a general AI system can learn from past experiences and improve itself, meaning that it doesn't have to be reprogrammed for every new task. In fact, there's no reason why an AGI system would need humans at all – once it learns enough, it could design its own machines or find ways to automate entire industries.

The advent of AI is transforming the business landscape and changing people's lives for the better. In the coming years, most industries will see a significant transformation due to new-age technologies like cloud computing, Internet of Things (IoT), and Big Data Analytics. All these factors profoundly influence how businesses operate today and are also finding applications in other areas like military, healthcare, and infrastructure development.

To build an engaging metaverse that appeals to millions of users who want to learn, create, and inhabit virtual worlds, AI must be used to enable realistic simulations of the real world. People need to feel immersed in the environments they participate in. AI is helping to achieve this reality by making objects look more realistic and enabling computer vision so users can interact with simulated objects using their body movements.

Concerns surrounding the advancement and usage of AI

AI is a very powerful idea, but it's not magic. The key thing to remember about AI is that it learns from data. The model and algorithm underneath are only as good as the data put into them. This means that data availability, bias, improper labeling, and privacy issues can all significantly impact the performance of an AI model.

Data availability and quality are critical for training an AI system. Some of the biggest concerns surrounding AI today relate to potentially biased datasets that may produce unsatisfactory results or exacerbate gender/racial biases within AI systems. When we research different types of machine learning models, we find that certain models are more susceptible to bias than others. For example, when using deep learning models (e.g., neural networks), the training process can introduce bias into the model if a biased dataset is used during training.

However, other machine learning models (e.g., random forests) can be less sensitive to the bias in the data during training. For example, if a dataset contains information about many different variables but only one variable is used to make decisions (e.g., gender), this model will tend to be more biased toward that variable than random forests that consider all variables equally weighted by default.

Other concerns need to be taken into account with the advancement and usage of AI. These include data availability, computational power, and privacy, such as health data. People's data is needed to develop models, but how do we get such data given how protected health data needs to be.

As artificial intelligence becomes more common, it's only natural that there are increasing requirements for processing power. As a result, AI researchers use supercomputers to develop algorithms and models on a massive and complex scale.

This is especially true of deep learning, a type of machine learning that uses algorithms to recognize patterns in large data sets like images or sound. The main issue with DL is that it requires enormous computational power. To train a neural network using DL, you need to feed vast amounts of data into the system — for example, thousands or millions of pictures — and then let it figure out how to tell one from another on its own. This training process is complex and laborious, but it is also computationally expensive. Model development can take days or even weeks on a single high-end GPU or CPU capable of delivering lots of computational power. To make matters worse, once you train the model, you need a supercomputer to execute the model at full capacity. Google's investments in TPUs (Tensor Processing Units) attempt to solve this problem using state-of-the-art hardware technology.

Another source of concern in the development of AI is how automated systems will ultimately be used. For example, should we consider holding corporations responsible for the actions of intelligent machines they develop? Or should we consider holding machine developers accountable for their work

What is artificial intelligence

While a number of definitions of artificial intelligence (AI) have surfaced over the last few decades, John McCarthy offers the following definition in this 2004 paper (link resides outside ibm.com), " It is the science and engineering of making intelligent machines, especially intelligent computer programs. It is related to the similar task of using computers to understand human intelligence, but AI does not have to confine itself to methods that are biologically observable."

However, decades before this definition, the birth of the artificial intelligence conversation was denoted by Alan Turing's seminal work, "Computing Machinery and Intelligence"(link resides outside ibm.com), which was published in 1950. In this paper, Turing, often referred to as the "father of computer science", asks the following question, "Can machines think?" From there, he offers a test, now famously known as the "Turing Test", where a human interrogator would try to distinguish between a computer and human text response. While this test has undergone much scrutiny since its publish, it remains an important part of the history of AI as well as an ongoing concept within philosophy as it utilizes ideas around linguistics.

Stuart Russell and Peter Norvig then proceeded to publish, Artificial Intelligence: A Modern Approach (link resides outside ibm.com), becoming one of the leading textbooks in the study of AI. In it, they delve into four potential goals or definitions of AI, which differentiates computer systems on the basis of rationality and thinking vs. acting:

Human approach:

Systems that think like humans

Systems that act like humans

Ideal approach:

Systems that think rationally

Systems that act rationally

Alan Turing's definition would have fallen under the category of "systems that act like humans."

At its simplest form, artificial intelligence is a field, which combines computer science and robust datasets, to enable problem-solving. It also encompasses sub-fields of machine learning and deep learning, which are frequently mentioned in conjunction with artificial intelligence. These disciplines are comprised of AI algorithms which seek to create expert systems which make predictions or classifications based on input data.

Over the years, artificial intelligence has gone through many cycles of hype, but even to skeptics, the release of OpenAI's ChatGPT seems to mark a turning point. The last time generative AI loomed this large, the breakthroughs were in computer vision, but now the leap forward is in natural language processing. And it's not just language: Generative models can also learn the grammar of software code, molecules, natural images, and a variety of other data types.

The applications for this technology are growing every day, and we're just starting to explore the possibilities. But as the hype around the use of AI in business takes off, conversations around ethics become critically important. To read more on where IBM stands within the conversation around AI ethics, read more here.

Types of artificial intelligence—weak AI vs. strong AI

Weak AI—also called Narrow AI or Artificial Narrow Intelligence (ANI)—is AI trained and focused to perform specific tasks. Weak AI drives most of the AI that surrounds us today. 'Narrow' might be a more accurate descriptor for this type of AI as it is anything but weak; it enables some very robust applications, such as Apple's Siri, Amazon's Alexa, IBM watson, and autonomous vehicles.

Strong AI is made up of Artificial General Intelligence (AGI) and Artificial Super Intelligence (ASI). Artificial general intelligence (AGI), or general AI, is a theoretical form of AI where a machine would have an intelligence equaled to humans; it would have a self-aware consciousness that has the ability to solve problems, learn, and plan for the future. Artificial Super Intelligence (ASI)—also known as superintelligence—would surpass the intelligence and ability of the human brain. While strong AI is still entirely theoretical with no practical examples in use today, that doesn't mean AI researchers aren't also exploring its development. In the meantime, the best examples of ASI might be from science fiction, such as HAL, the superhuman, rogue computer assistant in 2001: A Space Odyssey.

Deep learning vs. machine learning

Since deep learning and machine learning tend to be used interchangeably, it's worth noting the nuances between the two. As mentioned above, both deep learning and machine learning are sub-fields of artificial intelligence, and deep learning is actually a sub-field of machine learning.

Deep learning is actually comprised of neural networks. "Deep" in deep learning refers to a neural network comprised of more than three layers—which would be inclusive of the inputs and the output—can be considered a deep learning algorithm. This is generally represented using the diagram below.

The way in which deep learning and machine learning differ is in how each algorithm learns. Deep learning automates much of the feature extraction piece of the process, eliminating some of the manual human intervention required and enabling the use of larger data sets. You can think of deep learning as "scalable machine learning" as Lex Fridman noted in same MIT lecture from above. Classical, or "non-deep", machine learning is more dependent on human intervention to learn. Human experts determine the hierarchy of features to understand the differences between data inputs, usually requiring more structured data to learn.

"Deep" machine learning can leverage labeled datasets, also known as supervised learning, to inform its algorithm, but it doesn't necessarily require a labeled dataset. It can ingest unstructured data in its raw form (e.g. text, images), and it can automatically determine the hierarchy of features which distinguish different categories of data from one another. Unlike machine learning, it doesn't require human intervention to process data, allowing us to scale machine learning in more interesting ways.

The rise of generative models

Generative AI refers to deep-learning models that can take raw data — say, all of Wikipedia or the collected works of Rembrandt — and "learn" to generate statistically probable outputs when prompted. At a high level, generative models encode a simplified

representation of their training data and draw from it to create a new work that's similar,

but not identical, to the original data.

Generative models have been used for years in statistics to analyze numerical data. The rise of deep learning, however, made it possible to extend them to images, speech, and other complex data types. Among the first class of models to achieve this cross-over feat were variational autoencoders, or VAEs, introduced in 2013. VAEs were the first deep-learning models to be widely used for generating realistic images and speech.

"VAEs opened the floodgates to deep generative modeling by making models easier to

scale," said Akash Srivastava, an expert on generative AI at the MIT-IBM Watson AI Lab.

"Much of what we think of today as generative AI started here."

Early examples of models, like GPT-3, BERT, or DALL-E 2, have shown what's possible. The future is models that are trained on a broad set of unlabeled data that can be used for different tasks, with minimal fine-tuning. Systems that execute specific tasks in a single domain are giving way to broad AI that learns more generally and works across domains and problems. Foundation models, trained on large, unlabeled datasets and fine-tuned for an array of applications, are driving this shift.

When it comes to generative AI, it is predicted that foundation models will dramatically

accelerate AI adoption in enterprise. Reducing labeling requirements will make it much

easier for businesses to dive in, and the highly accurate, efficient AI-driven automation they enable will mean that far more companies will be able to deploy AI in a wider range of mission-critical situations. For IBM, the hope is that the power of foundation models can eventually be brought to every enterprise in a frictionless hybrid-cloud environment.

Artificial intelligence applications

There are numerous, real-world applications of AI systems today. Below are some of the most common use cases:

Speech recognition: It is also known as automatic speech recognition (ASR), computer speech recognition, or speech-to-text, and it is a capability which uses natural language processing (NLP) to process human speech into a written format. Many mobile devices incorporate speech recognition into their systems to conduct voice search—e.g. Siri—or provide more accessibility around texting.

Customer service: Online virtual agents are replacing human agents along the customer journey. They answer frequently asked questions (FAQs) around topics, like shipping, or provide personalized advice, cross-selling products or suggesting sizes for users, changing the way we think about customer engagement across websites and social media platforms. Examples include messaging bots on e-commerce sites with virtual agents, messaging apps, such as Slack and Facebook Messenger, and tasks usually done by virtual assistants and voice assistants.

Computer vision: This AI technology enables computers and systems to derive meaningful information from digital images, videos and other visual inputs, and based on those inputs, it can take action. This ability to provide recommendations distinguishes it from image recognition tasks. Powered by convolutional neural networks, computer vision has applications within photo tagging in social media, radiology imaging in healthcare, and self-driving cars within the automotive industry.

Recommendation engines: Using past consumption behavior data, AI algorithms can help to discover data trends that can be used to develop more effective cross-selling strategies. This is used to make relevant add-on recommendations to customers during the checkout process for online retailers.

Automated stock trading: Designed to optimize stock portfolios, AI-driven high-frequency trading platforms make thousands or even millions of trades per day without human intervention.

History of artificial intelligence: Key dates and names

The idea of 'a machine that thinks' dates back to ancient Greece. But since the advent of electronic computing (and relative to some of the topics discussed in this article) important events and milestones in the evolution of artificial intelligence include the following:

1950: Alan Turing publishes Computing Machinery and Intelligence. In the paper, Turing—famous for breaking the Nazi's ENIGMA code during WWII—proposes to answer the question 'can machines think?' and introduces the Turing Test to determine if a computer can demonstrate the same intelligence (or the results of the same intelligence) as a human. The value of the Turing test has been debated ever since.

1956: John McCarthy coins the term 'artificial intelligence' at the first-ever AI conference at Dartmouth College. (McCarthy would go on to invent the Lisp language.) Later that year, Allen Newell, J.C. Shaw, and Herbert Simon create the Logic Theorist, the first-ever running AI software program.

1967: Frank Rosenblatt builds the Mark 1 Perceptron, the first computer based on a neural network that 'learned' though trial and error. Just a year later, Marvin Minsky and Seymour Papert publish a book titled Perceptrons, which becomes both the landmark work on neural networks and, at least for a while, an argument against future neural network research projects.

1980s: Neural networks which use a backpropagation algorithm to train itself become widely used in AI applications.

1997: IBM's Deep Blue beats then world chess champion Garry Kasparov, in a chess match (and rematch).

2011: IBM watson beats champions Ken Jennings and Brad Rutter at Jeopardy!

2015: Baidu's Minwa supercomputer uses a special kind of deep neural network called a convolutional neural network to identify and categorize images with a higher rate of accuracy than the average human.

2016: DeepMind's AlphaGo program, powered by a deep neural network, beats Lee Sodol, the world champion Go player, in a five-game match. The victory is significant given the huge number of possible moves as the game progresses (over 14.5 trillion after just four moves!). Later, Google purchased DeepMind for a reported USD 400 million.

2023: A rise in large language models, or LLMs, such as ChatGPT, create an

enormous change in performance of AI and its potential to drive enterprise value.

With these new generative AI practices, deep-learning models can be pre-trained on

vast amounts of raw, unlabeled data.

Artificial Intelligence (AI) — Top 3 Pros and Cons

Pro 1

AI can make everyday life more convenient and enjoyable, improving our health and standard of living.

Why sit in a traffic jam when a map app can navigate you around the car accident? Why fumble with shopping bags searching for your keys in the dark when a preset location-based command can have your doorway illuminated as you approach your now unlocked door?

Why scroll through hundreds of possible TV shows when the streaming app already knows what genres you like? Why forget eggs at the grocery store when a digital assistant can take an inventory of your refrigerator and add them to your grocery list and have them delivered to your home? All of these marvels are assisted by AI technology.

AI-enabled fitness apps boomed during the COVID-19 pandemic when gyms were closed, increasing the number of AI options for at-home workouts. Now, you can not only set a daily steps goal with encouragement reminders on your smart watch, but you can ride through the countryside on a Peloton bike from your garage or have a personal trainer on your living room TV. For more specialized fitness, AI wearables can monitor yoga poses or golf and baseball swings.

AI can even enhance your doctor's appointments and medical procedures. It can alert medical caregivers to patterns in your health data as compared to the vast library of medical data, while also doing the paperwork tied to medical appointments so doctors have more time to focus on their patients, resulting in more personalized care. AI can even help surgeons be quicker, more accurate, and more minimally invasive in their operations.

Smart speakers including Amazon's Echo can use AI to soothe babies to sleep and monitor their breathing. Using AI, speakers can also detect regular and irregular heartbeats, as well as heart attacks and congestive heart failure.

Pro 2

AI can offer accessibility for people with disabilities.

Artificial intelligence is commonly integrated into smartphones and other household devices. Virtual assistants, including Siri, Alexa, and Cortana, can perform innumerable tasks from making a phone call to navigating the internet. Those who are deaf and hearing impaired can access transcripts of voicemails or other audio, for example.

Other virtual assistants can transcribe conversations as they happen, allowing for more comprehension and participation by those who are communicationally challenged. Using voice commands with virtual assistants can allow better use by people with dexterity disabilities who may have difficulty navigating small buttons or screens, or turning on a lamp.

Apps enabled by AI on smartphones and other devices, including VoiceOver and TalkBack, can read messages, describe app icons or images, and give information such as battery levels for visually impaired people. Other apps, such as Voiceitt, can transcribe and standardize the voices of people with speech impediments.

Wheelmap provides users with information about wheelchair accessibility. And Evelity offers users indoor navigation tools that are customized to the user's needs, providing audio or text instructions and routes for wheelchair accessibility.

Other AI implementations such as smart thermostats, smart lighting, and smart plugs can be automated to work on a schedule to aid people with mobility or cognitive disabilities lead more independent lives.

More advanced AI projects can combine with robotics to help physically disabled people. HOOBOX Robotics, for example, uses facial recognition software to allow a wheelchair user to move the wheelchair with facial expressions, making movement easier for seniors and those with ALS or quadriparesis.

Pro 3

Artificial intelligence can improve workplace safety.

AI doesn't get stressed, tired, or sick, three major causes of human accidents in the workplace. AI robots can collaborate with or replace humans for especially dangerous tasks. For example, 50% of construction companies that used drones to inspect roofs and other risky tasks saw improvements in safety.

Artificial intelligence can also help humans be more safe. For instance, AI can ensure employees are up-to-date on training by tracking and automatically scheduling safety or other training. AI can also check and offer corrections for ergonomics to prevent repetitive stress injuries or worse.

An AI program called AI-SAFE (Automated Intelligent System for Assuring Safe Working Environments) aims to automate the workplace personal protective equipment (PPE) check, eliminating human errors that could cause accidents in the workplace. With COVID-19 and more people wearing more PPE to prevent the spread of the virus, this sort of AI could protect against outbreaks.

In India, AI was used in the midst of the coronavirus pandemic to reopen factories safely by providing camera, cell phone, and smart wearable device-based technology to ensure social distancing, take employee temperatures at regular intervals, and perform contact tracing if anyone tested positive for the virus.

AI can also perform more sensitive harm-reduction tasks in the workplace such as scanning work emails for improper behavior and types of harassment.

Con 1

AI will harm the standard of living for many people by causing mass unemployment as robots replace people.

AI robots and other software and hardware are becoming less expensive and need none of the benefits and services required by human workers, such as sick days, lunch hours, bathroom breaks, health insurance, pay raises, promotions, and performance reviews, which spells trouble for workers and society at large.

48% of experts believed AI will replace a large number of blue- and even white-collar jobs, creating greater income inequality, increased unemployment, and a breakdown of the social order.

The axiom "everything that can be automated, will be automated" is no longer science fiction. Self-checkout kiosks in stores like CVS, Target, and WalMart use AI-assisted video and scanners to prevent theft, alert staff to suspicious transactions, predict shopping trends, and mitigate sticking points at checkout.These AI-enabled machines have displaced human cashiers. About 11,000 retail jobs were lost in 2019, largely due to self-checkout and other technologies. In 2020, during the COVID-19 pandemic, a self-checkout manufacturer shipped 25% more units globally, reflecting the more than 70% of American grocery shoppers who preferred self or touchless checkouts.

An Oct. 2020 World Economic Forum report found 43% of businesses surveyed planned to reduce workforces in favor of automation. Many businesses, especially fast-food restaurants, retail shops, and hotels, automated jobs during the COVID-19 pandemic.

Income inequality was exacerbated over the last four decades as 50-70% of changes in American paychecks were caused by wage decreases for workers whose industries experienced rapid automation, including AI technologies.

Con 2

AI repeats and exacerbates human racism.

Facial recognition has been found to be racially biased, easily recognizing the faces of white men while wrongly identifying black women 35% of the time. One study of Amazon's Rekognition AI program falsely matched 28 members of the US Congress with mugshots from a criminal database. 40% of the errors were people of color.

AI has also been disproportionately employed against black and brown communities, with more federal and local police surveillance cameras in neighborhoods of color, and more social media surveillance of Black Lives Matter and other black activists. The same technologies are used for housing and employment decisions and TSA airport screenings. Some cities, including Boston and San Francisco, have banned police use of facial recognition for these reasons.

One particular AI software tasked with predicting recidivism risk for US courts–the Correctional Offender Management Profiling for Alternative Sanctions (Compas)–was found to falsely label black defendants as high risk at twice the rate of white defenders, and to falsely label white defendants as low risk more often.

In China, facial recognition AI has been used to track Uyghurs, a largely Muslim minority. The US and other governments have accused the Chinese government of genocide and forced labor in Xinjiang where a large population of Uyghurs live.

Beyond facial recognition, online AI algorithms frequently fail to recognize and censor racial slurs, such as a recent incident in an Amazon product description for a black doll. AI is also incapable of distinguishing between when the N-word is being used as a slur and when it's being used culturally by a black person. AI algorithms have also been found to show a "persistent anti-Muslim bias," by associating violence with the word "Muslim" at a higher rate than with words describing other religions including Christians, Jews, Sikhs, or Buddhists.

Con 3

Artificial intelligence poses dangerous privacy risks.

Facial recognition technology can be used for passive, warrantless surveillance without knowledge of the person being watched. In Russia, facial recognition was used to monitor and arrest protesters who supported jailed opposition politician Alexei Navalny]. Russians fear a new facial recognition payment system for Moscow's metro will increase these sorts of arrests.

Ring, the AI doorbell company, partnered with more than 400 police departments as of 2019, allowing the police to request footage from users' doorbell cameras. While users were allowed to deny access to any footage, privacy experts fear the close relationship between Ring and the police could override customer privacy, especially when the doorbells frequently record others' property.

AI also follows you on your weekly errands. Target used an algorithm to determine which shoppers were pregnant and sent them baby- and pregnancy-specific coupons in the mail, infringing on the medical privacy of those who may be pregnant, as well as those whose shopping patterns may just imitate pregnant people.

Moreover, artificial intelligence can be a godsend to crooks. In 2020, a group of 17 criminals defrauded $35 million from a bank in the United Arab Emirates using AI "deep voice" technology to impersonate an employee authorized to make money transfers. In 2019, thieves attempted to steal $240,000 using the same AI technology to impersonate the CEO of an energy firm in the United Kingdom.

Best Examples Of How AI Is Already Used In Our Everyday Life

When you hear news about artificial intelligence (AI), it might be easy to assume it has nothing to do with you. You might imagine that artificial intelligence is only something the big tech giants are focused on, and that AI doesn't impact your everyday life. In reality, artificial intelligence is encountered by most people from morning until night. Here are 10 of the best examples of how AI is already used in our everyday lives.

1. Open your phone with face ID

One of the first things many people do each morning is to reach for their smartphones. And, when your device gets unlocked using biometrics such as with face ID, it's using artificial intelligence to enable that functionality. Apple's FaceID can see in 3D. It lights up your face and places 30,000 invisible infrared dots on it and captures an image. It then uses machine learning algorithms to compare the scan of your face with what it has stored about your face to determine if the person trying to unlock the phone is you or not. Apple states the chance of fooling FaceID is one in a million.

2. Social media

After unlocking their phones, what's next? Many people check out their social media accounts, including Facebook, Twitter, Instagram, and more, to get updated on what happened overnight. Not only is artificial intelligence working behind the scenes to personalize what you see on your feeds (because it's learned what types of posts most resonate with you based on past history), it's figuring out friend suggestions, identifying and filtering out fake news and machine learning is working to prevent cyberbullying.

3. Send an email or message

Every day most of us will send an email (or several). Tools such as Grammarly and spell check activate when you compose your email to help you draft messages free from errors. These tools use artificial intelligence and natural language processing. On the receiving end of your messages, spam filters use artificial intelligence to either block emails that are suspected as spam or identify an email as something your recipient would like to receive in their inbox. Anti-virus software uses machine learning as well to protect your email account.

4. Google search

Most of us can't go a day without searching Google for an answer or a product we can't live without. Search engines couldn't scan the entire internet and deliver what you want without the assistance of artificial intelligence. Those ads that seem to follow you around? Yep, those are enabled by AI, are based on your search history and are personalized to you with the goal of getting items in front of you that the algorithms believe you will value.

5. Digital voice assistants

From getting directions to your lunch spot to inquiring about the weather for your weekend getaway, digital voice assistants are quickly becoming our can't-live-without co-pilots through life. These tools from Siri and Alexa to Google Home and Cortana, use natural language processing and generators driven by AI to return answers to you.

6. Smart home devices

Our homes are increasingly becoming "smart." Many of us now have "smart" thermostats such as the Nest that learn about our heating/cooling preferences and daily habits to adjust the temperature to our liking in time for our return home. There are smart refrigerators that create lists for what you need based on what's no longer in your fridge, as well as offer wine recommendations that would go with your dinner. Of course, smart appliances will continue to be more common.

7. Commuting to work

The travel aids enabled by artificial intelligence include more than maps. Google maps and other travel apps use AI to monitor traffic to give you real-time traffic and weather conditions as well as suggest ways to avoid gridlock. The car you drive to work might have driver-assist technology, and in places such as Mountain View, California, you can request a self-driving car through Google's sister company Waymo to drive you to and from work.

8. Banking

There are many ways artificial intelligence is deployed in our banking system. It's highly involved in the security of our transactions and to detect fraud. If you deposit a check by scanning it with your phone, get a low-balance alert, or even log on to your online banking account, AI is at work behind the scenes. If you visit a shop at lunch and purchase a new pair of pants, artificial intelligence will verify the purchase to determine if it's a "normal" transaction to either validate or decline the transaction for fear someone unauthorized is using your credit card.

9. Amazon recommendations

Speaking of shopping, America's largest online retailer Amazon is another way many people are exposed to artificial intelligence regularly. The retailer's AI algorithms learned what you like and what other people who are like you purchased to deliver to your Amazon feed recommendations for what you might like in your carts. Amazon is so confident in its predictive analytics and algorithms that it will ship products towards you even before you "click to buy" with its anticipatory shipping algorithm.

10. Netflix

At the end of the day, when it's time to kick back and relax, many of us turn to streaming services such as Netflix. The company's recommendation engine is powered by artificial intelligence and uses your past viewing history to deliver suggestions for what you might want to watch (including genres, actors, time periods, and more). Its tool gets as specific as what time of day you were watching and what you traditionally like during that timeframe. In fact, 80% of what we're watching is driven by Netflix's recommendations.

Soo, it will be hard to imagine any of our daily routines without the help of AI.

Applications of Artificial Intelligence

1. AI Application in E-Commerce

Personalized Shopping

Artificial Intelligence technology is used to create recommendation engines through which you can engage better with your customers. These recommendations are made in accordance with their browsing history, preference, and interests. It helps in improving your relationship with your customers and their loyalty towards your brand.

AI-Powered Assistants

Virtual shopping assistants and chatbots help improve the user experience while shopping online. Natural Language Processing is used to make the conversation sound as human and personal as possible. Moreover, these assistants can have real-time engagement with your customers. Did you know that on amazon.com, soon, customer service could be handled by chatbots?

Fraud Prevention

Credit card frauds and fake reviews are two of the most significant issues that E-Commerce companies deal with. By considering the usage patterns, AI can help reduce the possibility of credit card fraud taking place. Many customers prefer to buy a product or service based on customer reviews. AI can help identify and handle fake reviews.

2. Applications Of Artificial Intelligence in Education

Although the education sector is the one most influenced by humans, Artificial Intelligence has slowly begun to seep its roots into the education sector as well. Even in the education sector, this slow transition of Artificial Intelligence has helped increase productivity among faculties and helped them concentrate more on students than office or administration work.

Some of these applications in this sector include:

Administrative Tasks Automated to Aid Educators

Artificial Intelligence can help educators with non-educational tasks like task-related duties like facilitating and automating personalized messages to students, back-office tasks like grading paperwork, arranging and facilitating parent and guardian interactions, routine issue feedback facilitating, managing enrollment, courses, and HR-related topics.

Creating Smart Content

Digitization of content like video lectures, conferences, and textbook guides can be made using Artificial Intelligence. We can apply different interfaces like animations and learning content through customization for students from different grades.

Artificial Intelligence helps create a rich learning experience by generating and providing audio and video summaries and integral lesson plans.

Voice Assistants

Without even the direct involvement of the lecturer or the teacher, a student can access extra learning material or assistance through Voice Assistants. Through this, printing costs of temporary handbooks and also provide answers to very common questions easily.

Personalized Learning

Using top AI technologies, hyper-personalization techniques can be used to monitor students' data thoroughly, and habits, lesson plans, reminders, study guides, flash notes, frequency or revision, etc., can be easily generated.

3. Applications of Artificial Intelligence in Lifestyle

Artificial Intelligence has a lot of influence on our lifestyle. Let us discuss a few of them.

Autonomous Vehicles

Automobile manufacturing companies like Toyota, Audi, Volvo, and Tesla use machine learning to train computers to think and evolve like humans when it comes to driving in any environment and object detection to avoid accidents.

Spam Filters

The email that we use in our day-to-day lives has AI that filters out spam emails sending them to spam or trash folders, letting us see the filtered content only. The popular email provider, Gmail, has managed to reach a filtration capacity of approximately 99.9%.

Facial Recognition

Our favorite devices like our phones, laptops, and PCs use facial recognition techniques by using face filters to detect and identify in order to provide secure access. Apart from personal usage, facial recognition is a widely used Artificial Intelligence application even in high security-related areas in several industries.

Recommendation System

Various platforms that we use in our daily lives like e-commerce, entertainment websites, social media, video sharing platforms, like youtube, etc., all use the recommendation system to get user data and provide customized recommendations to users to increase engagement. This is a very widely used Artificial Intelligence application in almost all industries.

Also Read: How Does Artificial Intelligence (AI) Work and Its Applications

4. Applications of Artificial Intelligence in Navigation

Based on research from MIT, GPS technology can provide users with accurate, timely, and detailed information to improve safety. The technology uses a combination of Convolutional Neural Networks and Graph Neural Networks, which makes lives easier for users by automatically detecting the number of lanes and road types behind obstructions on the roads. AI is heavily used by Uber and many logistics companies to improve operational efficiency, analyze road traffic, and optimize routes.

5. Applications of Artificial Intelligence in Robotics

Robotics is another field where Artificial Intelligence applications are commonly used. Robots powered by AI use real-time updates to sense obstacles in its path and pre-plan its journey instantly.

It can be used for:

- Carrying goods in hospitals, factories, and warehouses
- Cleaning offices and large equipment
- Inventory management

6. Applications of Artificial Intelligence in Human Resource

Did you know that companies use intelligent software to ease the hiring process?

Artificial Intelligence helps with blind hiring. Using machine learning software, you can examine applications based on specific parameters. AI drive systems can scan job candidates' profiles, and resumes to provide recruiters an understanding of the talent pool they must choose from.

7. Applications of Artificial Intelligence in Healthcare

Artificial Intelligence finds diverse applications in the healthcare sector. AI applications are used in healthcare to build sophisticated machines that can detect diseases and identify cancer cells. Artificial Intelligence can help analyze chronic conditions with lab and other medical data to ensure early diagnosis. AI uses the combination of historical data and medical intelligence for the discovery of new drugs.

8. Applications of Artificial Intelligence in Agriculture

Artificial Intelligence is used to identify defects and nutrient deficiencies in the soil. This is done using computer vision, robotics, and machine learning applications, AI can analyze where weeds are growing. AI bots can help to harvest crops at a higher volume and faster pace than human laborers.

9. Applications of Artificial Intelligence in Gaming

Another sector where Artificial Intelligence applications have found prominence is the gaming sector. AI can be used to create smart, human-like NPCs to interact with the players.

It can also be used to predict human behavior using which game design and testing can be improved. The Alien Isolation game released in 2014 uses AI to stalk the player throughout the game. The game uses two Artificial Intelligence systems - 'Director AI' that frequently knows your location and the 'Alien AI,' driven by sensors and behaviors that continuously hunt the player.

10. Applications of Artificial Intelligence in Automobiles

Artificial Intelligence is used to build self-driving vehicles. AI can be used along with the vehicle's camera, radar, cloud services, GPS, and control signals to operate the vehicle. AI can improve the in-vehicle experience and provide additional systems like emergency braking, blind-spot monitoring, and driver-assist steering.

11. Applications of Artificial Intelligence in Social Media

Instagram

On Instagram, AI considers your likes and the accounts you follow to determine what posts you are shown on your explore tab.

Facebook

Artificial Intelligence is also used along with a tool called DeepText. With this tool, Facebook can understand conversations better. It can be used to translate posts from different languages automatically.

Twitter

AI is used by Twitter for fraud detection, for removing propaganda, and hateful content. Twitter also uses AI to recommend tweets that users might enjoy, based on what type of tweets they engage with.

12. Applications of Artificial Intelligence in Marketing

Artificial Intelligence (AI) applications are popular in the marketing domain as well.

Using AI, marketers can deliver highly targeted and personalized ads with the help of behavioral analysis, and pattern recognition in ML, etc. It also helps with retargeting audiences at the right time to ensure better results and reduced feelings of distrust and annoyance.

AI can help with content marketing in a way that matches the brand's style and voice. It can be used to handle routine tasks like performance, campaign reports, and much more.

Chatbots powered by AI, Natural Language Processing, Natural Language Generation, and Natural Language Understanding can analyze the user's language and respond in the ways humans do.

AI can provide users with real-time personalizations based on their behavior and can be used to edit and optimize marketing campaigns to fit a local market's needs.

13. Applications of Artificial Intelligence in Chatbots

AI chatbots can comprehend natural language and respond to people online who use the "live chat" feature that many organizations provide for customer service. AI chatbots are effective with the use of machine learning and can be integrated in an array of websites and applications. AI chatbots can eventually build a database of answers, in addition to pulling information from an established selection of integrated answers. As AI continues to improve, these chatbots can effectively resolve customer issues, respond to simple inquiries, improve customer service, and provide 24/7 support. All in all, these AI chatbots can help to improve customer satisfaction.

14. Applications of Artificial Intelligence in Finance

It has been reported that 80% of banks recognize the benefits that AI can provide. Whether it's personal finance, corporate finance, or consumer finance, the highly evolved technology that is offered through AI can help to significantly improve a wide range of financial services. For example, customers looking for help regarding wealth management solutions can easily get the information they need through SMS text messaging or online chat, all AI-powered. Artificial Intelligence can also detect changes in transaction patterns and other potential red flags that can signify fraud, which humans can easily miss, and thus saving businesses and individuals from significant loss. Aside from fraud detection and task automation, AI can also better predict and assess loan risks.

15. AI in Astronomy

If there's one concept that has caught everyone by storm in this beautiful world of technology, it has to be - AI (Artificial Intelligence), without a question. AI or Artificial Intelligence has seen a wide range of applications throughout the years, including healthcare, robotics, eCommerce, and even finance.

Astronomy, on the other hand, is a largely unexplored topic that is just as intriguing and thrilling as the rest. When it comes to astronomy, one of the most difficult problems is analyzing the data. As a result, astronomers are turning to machine learning and Artificial Intelligence (AI) to create new tools. Having said that, consider how Artificial Intelligence has altered astronomy and is meeting the demands of astronomers.

Recently, a group of scientists used Artificial Intelligence in a galaxy merger investigation to establish that galaxy mergers were the primary force underlying starbursts. Given the size of the collection, the researchers created a deep learning system that trained itself to locate merging galaxies. According to one of the astronomers, the advantage of Artificial Intelligence is that it improves the study's repeatability. The reason for this is that the algorithm's definitions of a merger are consistent.

The changing sky has captured everyone's attention as one of the most astounding projects of all time. This project seeks to survey the whole night sky every night, gathering over 80 terabytes of data in one go to study how stars and galaxies in the cosmos change over time.

One of the most important duties for an astronomer is to find a p. The theory is that whenever an exoplanet passes in front of its parent star, part of the light is blocked, which humans can see. Astronomers use this location to study an exoplanet's orbit and develop a picture of the light dips. They then identify the planet's many parameters, such as its mass, size, and distance from its star, to mention a few. However, AI proves to be more than a savior in this case. Using AI's time-series analysis capabilities, it is feasible to analyze data as a sequential sequence and identify planetary signals with up to 96% accuracy.

Finding the signals of the universe's most catastrophic events is critical for astronomers. When exoplanets collide with each other, they cause ripples in space-time. These can be identified further by monitoring feeble signals on Earth. Collaborations on gravitational-wave detectors - Ligo and Virgo have performed admirably in this regard. Both of them were effective in recognizing signals using machine learning. Astronomers now get notifications, allowing them to point their telescopes in the appropriate direction.

16. AI in Data Security

Many people believe that Artificial Intelligence (AI) is the present and future of the technology sector. Many industry leaders employ AI for a variety of purposes, including providing valued services and preparing their companies for the future.

Data security, which is one of the most important assets of any tech-oriented firm, is one of the most prevalent and critical applications of AI. With confidential data ranging from consumer data (such as credit card information) to organizational secrets kept online, data security is vital for any institution to satisfy both legal and operational duties. This work is now as difficult as it is vital, and many businesses deploy AI-based security solutions to keep their data out of the wrong hands.

Because the world is smarter and more connected than ever before, the function of Artificial Intelligence in business is critical today. According to several estimates, cyberattacks will get more tenacious over time, and security teams will need to rely on AI solutions to keep systems and data under control.

Identifies Unknown Threats

A human may not be able to recognize all of the hazards that a business confronts. Every year, hackers launch hundreds of millions of assaults for a variety of reasons. Unknown threats can cause severe network damage. Worse, they can have an impact before you recognize, identify, and prevent them.

As attackers test different tactics ranging from malware assaults to sophisticated malware assaults, contemporary solutions should be used to avoid them. Artificial Intelligence has shown to be one of the most effective security solutions for mapping and preventing unexpected threats from wreaking havoc on a corporation.

Flaw Identification

AI assists in detecting data overflow in a buffer. When programs consume more data than usual, this is referred to as buffer overflow. Aside from the fault caused by human triggers breaking crucial data. These blunders are also observable by AI, and they are detected in real-time, preventing future dangers.

AI can precisely discover cybersecurity weaknesses, faults, and other problems using Machine Learning. Machine Learning also assists AI in identifying questionable data provided by any application. Malware or virus used by hackers to gain access to systems as well as steal data is carried out via programming language flaws.

Threat Prevention

Artificial Intelligence technology is constantly being developed by cyber security vendors. In its advanced version, AI is designed to detect flaws in the system or even the update. It'd instantly exclude anybody attempting to exploit those issues. AI would be an outstanding tool for preventing any threat from occurring. It may install additional firewalls as well as rectify code faults that lead to dangers.

Responding to Threats

It's something that happens after the threat has entered the system. As previously explained, AI is used to detect unusual behavior and create an outline of viruses or malware. AI is currently taking appropriate action against viruses or malware. The reaction consists mostly of removing the infection, repairing the fault, and administering the harm done. Finally, AI guarantees that such an incident does not happen again and takes proper preventative actions.

Recognize Uncharacterised Action

AI allows us to detect unusual behavior in a system. It is capable of detecting unusual or unusual behavior by continually scanning a system and gathering an appropriate amount of data. In addition, AI identifies illegal access. When unusual behavior is identified, Artificial Intelligence employs particular elements to determine whether it represents a genuine threat or a fabricated warning. Machine Learning is used to help AI determine what is and is not aberrant behavior. Machine Learning is also improving with time, which will allow Artificial Intelligence to detect even minor anomalies. As a result, AI would point to anything wrong with the system.

17. AI in Travel and Transport

Intelligent technology has become a part of our daily lives in recent years. And, as technology advances across society, new uses of AI, notably in transportation, are becoming mainstream. This has created a new market for firms and entrepreneurs to develop innovative solutions for making public transportation more comfortable, accessible, and safe.

Intelligent transportation systems have the potential to become one of the most effective methods to improve the quality of life for people all around the world. There are multiple instances of similar systems in use in various sectors.

Heavy Goods Transportation

Truck platooning, which networks HGV (heavy goods vehicles), for example, might be extremely valuable for vehicle transport businesses or for moving other large items.

The lead vehicle in a truck platoon is steered by a human driver, however, the human drivers in any other trucks drive passively, just taking the wheel in exceptionally dangerous or difficult situations.

Because all of the trucks in the platoon are linked via a network, they travel in formation and activate the actions done by the human driver in the lead vehicle at the same time. So, if the lead driver comes to a complete stop, all of the vehicles following him do as well.

Traffic Management

Clogged city streets are a key impediment to urban transportation all around the world. Cities throughout the world have enlarged highways, erected bridges, and established other modes of transportation such as train travel, yet the traffic problem persists. However, AI advancements in traffic management provide a genuine promise of changing the situation.

Intelligent traffic management may be used to enforce traffic regulations and promote road safety. For example, Alibaba's City Brain initiative in China uses AI technologies such as predictive analysis, big data analysis, and a visual search engine in order to track road networks in real-time and reduce congestion.

Building a city requires an efficient transformation system, and AI-based traffic management technologies are powering next-generation smart cities.

Ride-Sharing

Platforms like Uber and OLA leverage AI to improve user experiences by connecting riders and drivers, improving user communication and messaging, and optimizing decision-making. For example, Uber has its own proprietary ML-as-a-service platform called Michelangelo that can anticipate supply and demand, identify trip abnormalities like wrecks, and estimate arrival timings.

Route Planning

AI-enabled route planning using predictive analytics may help both businesses and people. Ride-sharing services already achieve this by analyzing numerous real-world parameters to optimize route planning.

AI-enabled route planning is a terrific approach for businesses, particularly logistics and shipping industries, to construct a more efficient supply network by anticipating road conditions and optimizing vehicle routes. Predictive analytics in route planning is the intelligent evaluation by a machine of a number of road usage parameters such as congestion level, road restrictions, traffic patterns, consumer preferences, and so on.

Cargo logistics companies, such as vehicle transport services or other general logistics firms, may use this technology to reduce delivery costs, accelerate delivery times, and better manage assets and operations.

18. AI in Automotive Industry

A century ago, the idea of machines being able to comprehend, do complex computations, and devise efficient answers to pressing issues was more of a science fiction writer's vision than a predictive reality. Still, as we enter the third decade of the twenty-first century, we can't fathom our lives without stock trading and marketing bots, manufacturing robots, smart assistance, virtual travel agents, and other innovations made possible by advances in Artificial Intelligence and machine learning. The importance of Artificial Intelligence and machine learning in the automotive sector cannot be overstated.

With Artificial Intelligence driving more applications to the automotive sector, more businesses are deciding to implement Artificial Intelligence and machine learning models in production.

Manufacturing

Infusing AI into the production experience allows automakers to benefit from smarter factories, boosting productivity and lowering costs. AI may be utilized in automobile assembly, supply chain optimization, employing robots on the manufacturing floor, improving performance using sensors, designing cars, and in post-production activities.

Supply Chain

The automobile sector has been beset by supply chain interruptions and challenges in 2021 and 2022. AI can also assist in this regard. AI helps firms identify the hurdles they will face in the future by forecasting and replenishing supply chains as needed. AI may also assist with routing difficulties, volume forecasts, and other concerns.

Passenger and Driver Experience

We all wish to have a pleasant journey in our vehicles. Artificial Intelligence can also help with this. When driving, Artificial Intelligence (AI) may assist drivers in remaining focused by decreasing distractions, analyzing driving behaviors, and enhancing the entire customer experience. Passengers can benefit from customized accessibility as well as in-car delivery services thanks to AI.

Inspections

The procedure of inspecting an automobile by a rental agency, insurance provider, or even a garage is very subjective and manual. With AI, car inspection may go digital, with modern technology being able to analyze a vehicle, identify where the flaws are, and produce a thorough status report.

Quality Control

Everyone desires a premium vehicle and experience. Wouldn't you prefer to know if something is wrong with your automobile before it breaks down? In this application, AI enables extremely accurate predictive monitoring, fracture detection, and other functions.

Artificial Intelligence Effect on Human Application

Humans may appear to be swiftly overtaken in industries where AI is becoming more extensively incorporated. However, humans are still capable of doing a variety of complicated activities better than AI. For the time being, tasks that demand creativity are beyond the capabilities of AI computers.

For instance, a writer utilized AI to generate fresh screenplays for episodes of the TV sitcom 'Friends', all of which proved hard to read. While some authors are turning to AI writing tools for inspiration for their poetry and fiction, AI cannot handle all of the jobs for them.

Furthermore, while natural language processing has advanced significantly, AI is still not very adept at truly understanding the words that it reads. While language is frequently predictable enough that AI can participate in trustworthy communication in specific settings, unexpected phrases, irony, or subtlety might confound it. Similarly, AI cannot yet demonstrate empathy or critical reasoning. In comparison to AI, humans continue to excel in tasks that demand these talents.

AI has advanced swiftly and has become an essential component of our daily life. However, the day when AI will do everything for us and we will be able to spend our days resting or learning for pleasure is still a long way off. Artificial Intelligence still has to advance in areas such as language processing, creativity, problem-solving, and subtlety comprehension. If you're concerned that robots will take your job, build these qualities in yourself to ensure that you'll be employable in the future.

People leverage the strength of Artificial Intelligence because the work they need to carry out is rising on a daily basis. So automating everyday tasks is a smart idea. This saves the organization's staff while also increasing output. Furthermore, the organization may obtain competent individuals for the company's development through the use of Artificial Intelligence.

Also, businesses nowadays believe that they wish to automate all regular and ordinary tasks. And they believe they can automate such routine tasks using a simple application. Because automation is becoming more widespread as data science advances. This AI is most commonly used in online chat portals. You've undoubtedly seen the welcome message when you visit the websites. After that, the genuine talk generally begins.

Types of Artificial Intelligence

f you've ever used Amazon's Alexa, Apple's Face ID or interacted with a chatbot, you've interacted with artificial intelligence (AI) technology.

There are a lot of ongoing AI discoveries and developments, most of which are divided into different types. These classifications reveal more of a storyline than a taxonomy, one that can tell us how far AI has come, where it's going and what the future holds.

These are the seven types of AI to know, and what we can expect from the technology.

7 TYPES OF ARTIFICIAL INTELLIGENCE

1. Artificial Narrow Intelligence: AI designed to complete very specific actions; unable to independently learn.
2. Artificial General Intelligence: AI designed to learn, think and perform at similar levels to humans.
3. Artificial Superintelligence: AI able to surpass the knowledge and capabilities of humans.
4. Reactive Machines: AI capable of responding to external stimuli in real time; unable to build memory or store information for future.
5. Limited Memory: AI that can store knowledge and use it to learn and train for future tasks.
6. Theory of Mind: AI that can sense and respond to human emotions, plus perform the tasks of limited memory machines.

7. Self-aware: AI that can recognize others' emotions, plus has sense of self and human-level intelligence; the final stage of AI.

Capability-Based Types of Artificial Intelligence

Based on how they learn and how far they can apply their knowledge, all AI can be broken down into three capability types: Artificial narrow intelligence, artificial general intelligence and artificial superintelligence. Here's what to know about each.

1. ARTIFICIAL NARROW INTELLIGENCE

Artificial narrow intelligence (ANI), also known as narrow AI or weak AI, describes AI tools designed to carry out very specific actions or commands. ANI technologies are built to serve and excel in one cognitive capability, and cannot independently learn skills beyond its design. They often utilize machine learning and neural network algorithms to complete these specified tasks.

For instance, natural language processing AI is a type of narrow intelligence because it can recognize and respond to voice commands, but cannot perform other tasks beyond that.

Some examples of artificial narrow intelligence include image recognition software, self-driving cars and AI virtual assistants like Siri.

2. ARTIFICIAL GENERAL INTELLIGENCE

Artificial general intelligence (AGI), also called general AI or strong AI, describes AI that can learn, think and perform a wide range of actions similarly to humans. The goal of designing artificial general intelligence is to be able to create machines that are capable of performing multifunctional tasks and act as lifelike, equally intelligent assistants to humans in everyday life.

Though still a work in progress, the groundwork of artificial general intelligence could be built from technologies such as supercomputers, quantum hardware and generative AI models like ChatGPT.

3. ARTIFICIAL SUPERINTELLIGENCE

Artificial superintelligence (ASI), or super AI, is the stuff of science fiction. It's theorized that once AI has reached the general intelligence level, it will soon learn at such a fast rate that its knowledge and capabilities will become stronger than that even of humankind.

ASI would act as the backbone technology of completely self-aware AI and other individualistic robots. Its concept is also what fuels the popular media trope of "AI takeovers," as seen in films like Ex Machina or I, Robot. But at this point, it's all speculation.

"Artificial superintelligence will become by far the most capable forms of intelligence on earth," said David Rogenmoser, CEO of AI writing company Jasper. "It will have the intelligence of human beings and will be exceedingly better at everything that we do."

4 Types of Machine Learning to Know

Functionality-Based Types of Artificial Intelligence

Functionality concerns how an AI applies its learning capabilities to process data, respond to stimuli and interact with its environment. As such, AI can be sorted by four functionality types.

4. REACTIVE MACHINES

The genesis of AI began with the development of reactive machines, the most fundamental type of AI. Reactive machines are just that — reactionary. They can respond to immediate requests and tasks, but they aren't capable of storing memory or learning from past experiences.

"They cannot improve their functionality through experience, and can only respond to a limited combination of inputs."

In practice, reactive machines can read and respond to external stimuli in real time. This makes them useful for performing basic autonomous functions, such as filtering spam from your email inbox or recommending movies based on your most recent Netflix searches.

Most famously, IBM's reactive AI machine Deep Blue was able to read real-time cues in order to beat Russian chess grandmaster Garry Kasparov in a 1997 chess match. But beyond that, reactive AI can't build upon previous knowledge or perform more complex tasks. In order to apply AI in more advanced scenarios, developments in data storage and memory management needed to occur.

5. LIMITED MEMORY

The next step in AI's evolution is developing a capacity for storing knowledge. But it would be nearly three decades before that breakthrough was reached, according to Rafael Tena, senior AI researcher at insurance company Acrisure Innovation.

"All present-day AI systems are trained by large volumes of training data that they store in their memory to form a reference model for solving future problems."

"There was a huge amount of progress in the 80s," Tena said. But that eventually slowed. "There were small incremental changes …until deep learning came around."

In 2012, the field of AI made major progress. New innovations from Google and Image Net made it possible for artificial intelligence to store past data and make predictions using it. This type of AI is referred to as limited memory AI, because it can build its own limited knowledge base and use that knowledge to improve over time. Today, the limited memory model represents the majority of AI applications.

"Nearly all existing applications that we know of come under this category of AI," Rogenmoser said. "All present-day AI systems are trained by large volumes of training data that they store in their memory to form a reference model for solving future problems."

Limited memory AI can be applied in a broad range of scenarios, from smaller scale applications, such as chatbots, to self-driving cars and other advanced use cases.

6. THEORY OF MIND

In terms of AI's progress, limited memory technology is the furthest we've come — but it's not the final destination. Limited memory machines can learn from past experiences and store knowledge, but they can't pick up on subtle environmental changes, emotional cues or reach the same level of human intelligence.

"Current models have a one-way relationship," Rogenmoser said. "AI [tools] like Alexa and Siri don't react with any emotional support when you yell at them."

The concept of AI that can perceive and pick up on the emotions of others hasn't been fully realized yet. This concept is referred to as "theory of mind," a term borrowed from psychology that describes humans' ability to read the emotions of others and predict future actions based on that information.

"Machines may work better than us 90 percent of the time, but that last ten percent, what you would describe as common sense, is really hard to get to."

Tena provided an example to illustrate how a successful theory of mind application would revolutionize the technology: A self-driving car may perform better than a human driver the majority of the time because it won't make the same human errors. But if you, as a driver, know that your neighbor's kid tends to play close to the street after school, you'll know instinctively to slow down while passing that neighbor's driveway — something an AI vehicle equipped with basic limited memory wouldn't be able to do.

Theory of mind could bring plenty of positive changes to the tech world, but it also poses its own risks. Since emotional cues are so nuanced, it would take a long time for AI machines to perfect reading them, and could potentially make big errors while in the learning stage. Some people also fear that once technologies are able to respond to emotional signals as well as situational ones, the result could mean automation of some jobs. But no need to worry just yet — Rogenmoser said that this hypothetical future, however, is still very far off.

"Right now, this intelligence is science fiction," he said. "We're not even close to developing this type of AI, so no one is getting their job stolen by AI."

7. SELF-AWARE

The stage beyond theory of mind, when artificial intelligence develops self awareness, is referred to as the AI point of singularity. It's thought that once that point is reached, AI machines will be beyond our control, because they'll not only be able to sense the feelings of others, but will have a sense of self as well.

"People both strive to create this type of AI and fear the consequences of its creation, worrying that this type of AI could steal our jobs or take over our world," Rogenmoser said. "If this type of AI is successfully created, no one knows what the impact will be."

"If this type of AI is successfully created, no one knows what the impact will be."

Steps are being taken by researchers and engineers to develop rudimentary versions of self-aware AI. Perhaps one of the most famous of these is Sophia, a robot developed by robotics company Hanson Robotics.

While not technically self aware, Sophia's advanced application of current AI technologies provides a glimpse of AI's potentially self-aware future. It's a future of promise as well as danger — and there's debate about whether it's ethical to build sentient AI at all. But for now, Rogenmoser said we don't need to worry about AI conquering the world.

"AI is going to become much better at solving real use cases, but I want to express that I don't think this [means] the end of humans and the end of work," he said. "We will continue to see AI pop up in useful ways to amplify the great work that people are already doing."

Risks and Dangers of Artificial Intelligence (AI)

As AI grows more sophisticated and widespread, the voices warning against the potential dangers of artificial intelligence grow louder.

"These things could get more intelligent than us and could decide to take over, and we need to worry now about how we prevent that happening," said Geoffrey Hinton, known as the "Godfather of AI" for his foundational work on machine learning and neural network algorithms. In 2023, Hinton left his position at Google so that he could "talk about the dangers of AI," noting a part of him even regrets his life's work.

The renowned computer scientist isn't alone in his concerns.

Tesla and SpaceX founder Elon Musk, along with over 1,000 other tech leaders, urged in a 2023 open letter to put a pause on large AI experiments, citing that the technology can "pose profound risks to society and humanity."

RISKS OF ARTIFICIAL INTELLIGENCE

- Automation-spurred job loss
- Deepfakes
- Privacy violations
- Algorithmic bias caused by bad data
- Socioeconomic inequality
- Market volatility
- Weapons automatization
- Uncontrollable self-aware AI

Whether it's the increasing automation of certain jobs, gender and racially biased algorithms or autonomous weapons that operate without human oversight (to name just a few), unease abounds on a number of fronts. And we're still in the very early stages of what AI is really capable of.

1. LACK OF AI TRANSPARENCY AND EXPLAINABILITY

AI and deep learning models can be difficult to understand, even for those that work directly with the technology. This leads to a lack of transparency for how and why AI comes to its conclusions, creating a lack of explanation for what data AI algorithms use, or why they may make biased or unsafe decisions. These concerns have given rise to the use of explainable AI, but there's still a long way before transparent AI systems become common practice.

2. JOB LOSSES DUE TO AI AUTOMATION

AI-powered job automation is a pressing concern as the technology is adopted in industries like marketing, manufacturing and healthcare. By 2030, tasks that account for up to 30 percent of hours currently being worked in the U.S. economy could be automated — with Black and Hispanic employees left especially vulnerable to the change — according to McKinsey. Goldman Sachs even states 300 million full-time jobs could be lost to AI automation.

"The reason we have a low unemployment rate, which doesn't actually capture people that aren't looking for work, is largely that lower-wage service sector jobs have been pretty robustly created by this economy," futurist Martin Ford told Built In. With AI on the rise, though, "I don't think that's going to continue."

As AI robots become smarter and more dexterous, the same tasks will require fewer humans. And while AI is estimated to create 97 million new jobs by 2025, many employees won't have the skills needed for these technical roles and could get left behind if companies don't upskill their workforces.

"If you're flipping burgers at McDonald's and more automation comes in, is one of these new jobs going to be a good match for you?" Ford said. "Or is it likely that the new job requires lots of education or training or maybe even intrinsic talents — really strong interpersonal skills or creativity — that you might not have? Because those are the things that, at least so far, computers are not very good at."

Even professions that require graduate degrees and additional post-college training aren't immune to AI displacement.

As technology strategist Chris Messina has pointed out, fields like law and accounting are primed for an AI takeover. In fact, Messina said, some of them may well be decimated. AI already is having a significant impact on medicine. Law and accounting are next, Messina said, the former being poised for "a massive shakeup."

"Think about the complexity of contracts, and really diving in and understanding what it takes to create a perfect deal structure," he said in regards to the legal field. "It's a lot of attorneys reading through a lot of information — hundreds or thousands of pages of data and documents. It's really easy to miss things. So AI that has the ability to comb through and comprehensively deliver the best possible contract for the outcome you're trying to achieve is probably going to replace a lot of corporate attorneys."

3. SOCIAL MANIPULATION THROUGH AI ALGORITHMS

Social manipulation also stands as a danger of artificial intelligence. This fear has become a reality as politicians rely on platforms to promote their viewpoints, with one example being Ferdinand Marcos, Jr., wielding a TikTok troll army to capture the votes of younger Filipinos during the Philippines' 2022 election.

TikTok, which is just one example of a social media platform that relies on AI algorithms, fills a user's feed with content related to previous media they've viewed on the platform. Criticism of the app targets this process and the algorithm's failure to filter out harmful and inaccurate content, raising concerns over TikTok's ability to protect its users from misleading information.

Online media and news have become even murkier in light of AI-generated images and videos, AI voice changers as well as deepfakes infiltrating political and social spheres. These technologies make it easy to create realistic photos, videos, audio clips or replace the image of one figure with another in an existing picture or video. As a result, bad actors have another avenue for sharing misinformation and war propaganda, creating a nightmare scenario where it can be nearly impossible to distinguish between creditable and faulty news.

"No one knows what's real and what's not," Ford said. "So it really leads to a situation where you literally cannot believe your own eyes and ears; you can't rely on what, historically, we've considered to be the best possible evidence... That's going to be a huge issue."

4. SOCIAL SURVEILLANCE WITH AI TECHNOLOGY

In addition to its more existential threat, Ford is focused on the way AI will adversely affect privacy and security. A prime example is China's use of facial recognition technology in offices, schools and other venues. Besides tracking a person's movements, the Chinese government may be able to gather enough data to monitor a person's activities, relationships and political views.

Another example is U.S. police departments embracing predictive policing algorithms to anticipate where crimes will occur. The problem is that these algorithms are influenced by arrest rates, which disproportionately impact Black communities. Police departments then double down on these communities, leading to over-policing and questions over whether self-proclaimed democracies can resist turning AI into an authoritarian weapon.

"Authoritarian regimes use or are going to use it," Ford said. "The question is, How much does it invade Western countries, democracies, and what constraints do we put on it?"

5. LACK OF DATA PRIVACY USING AI TOOLS

If you've played around with an AI chatbot or tried out an AI face filter online, your data is being collected — but where is it going and how is it being used? AI systems often collect personal data to customize user experiences or to help train the AI models you're using (especially if the AI tool is free). Data may not even be considered secure from other users when given to an AI system, as one bug incident that occurred with ChatGPT in 2023 "allowed some users to see titles from another active user's chat history." While there are laws present to protect personal information in some cases in the United States, there is no explicit federal law that protects citizens from data privacy harm experienced by AI.

6. BIASES DUE TO AI

Various forms of AI bias are detrimental too. Speaking to the New York Times, Princeton computer science professor Olga Russakovsky said AI bias goes well beyond gender and race. In addition to data and algorithmic bias (the latter of which can "amplify" the former), AI is developed by humans — and humans are inherently biased.

"A.I. researchers are primarily people who are male, who come from certain racial demographics, who grew up in high socioeconomic areas, primarily people without disabilities," Russakovsky said. "We're a fairly homogeneous population, so it's a challenge to think broadly about world issues."

The limited experiences of AI creators may explain why speech-recognition AI often fails to understand certain dialects and accents, or why companies fail to consider the consequences of a chatbot impersonating notorious figures in human history. Developers and businesses should exercise greater care to avoid recreating powerful biases and prejudices that put minority populations at risk.

7. SOCIOECONOMIC INEQUALITY AS A RESULT OF AI

If companies refuse to acknowledge the inherent biases baked into AI algorithms, they may compromise their DEI initiatives through AI-powered recruiting. The idea that AI can measure the traits of a candidate through facial and voice analyses is still tainted by racial biases, reproducing the same discriminatory hiring practices businesses claim to be eliminating.

Widening socioeconomic inequality sparked by AI-driven job loss is another cause for concern, revealing the class biases of how AI is applied. Blue-collar workers who perform more manual, repetitive tasks have experienced wage declines as high as 70 percent because of automation. Meanwhile, white-collar workers have remained largely untouched, with some even enjoying higher wages.

Sweeping claims that AI has somehow overcome social boundaries or created more jobs fail to paint a complete picture of its effects. It's crucial to account for differences based on race, class and other categories. Otherwise, discerning how AI and automation benefit certain individuals and groups at the expense of others becomes more difficult.

8. WEAKENING ETHICS AND GOODWILL BECAUSE OF AI

Along with technologists, journalists and political figures, even religious leaders are sounding the alarm on AI's potential socio-economic pitfalls. In a 2019 Vatican meeting titled, "The Common Good in the Digital Age," Pope Francis warned against AI's ability to "circulate tendentious opinions and false data" and stressed the far-reaching consequences of letting this technology develop without proper oversight or restraint.

"If mankind's so-called technological progress were to become an enemy of the common good," he added, "this would lead to an unfortunate regression to a form of barbarism dictated by the law of the strongest."

The rapid rise of generative AI tools like ChatGPT and Bard gives these concerns more substance. Many users have applied the technology to get out of writing assignments, threatening academic integrity and creativity.

Some fear that, no matter how many powerful figures point out the dangers of artificial intelligence, we're going to keep pushing the envelope with it if there's money to be made.

"The mentality is, 'If we can do it, we should try it; let's see what happens," Messina said. "'And if we can make money off it, we'll do a whole bunch of it.' But that's not unique to technology. That's been happening forever.'"

9. AUTONOMOUS WEAPONS POWERED BY AI

As is too often the case, technological advancements have been harnessed for the purpose of warfare. When it comes to AI, some are keen to do something about it before it's too late: In a 2016 open letter, over 30,000 individuals, including AI and robotics researchers, pushed back against the investment in AI-fueled autonomous weapons.

"The key question for humanity today is whether to start a global AI arms race or to prevent it from starting," they wrote. "If any major military power pushes ahead with AI weapon development, a global arms race is virtually inevitable, and the endpoint of this technological trajectory is obvious: autonomous weapons will become the Kalashnikovs of tomorrow."

This prediction has come to fruition in the form of Lethal Autonomous Weapon Systems, which locate and destroy targets on their own while abiding by few regulations. Because of the proliferation of potent and complex weapons, some of the world's most powerful nations have given in to anxieties and contributed to a tech cold war.

Many of these new weapons pose major risks to civilians on the ground, but the danger becomes amplified when autonomous weapons fall into the wrong hands. Hackers have mastered various types of cyber attacks, so it's not hard to imagine a malicious actor infiltrating autonomous weapons and instigating absolute armageddon.

If political rivalries and warmongering tendencies are not kept in check, artificial intelligence could end up being applied with the worst intentions.

10. FINANCIAL CRISES BROUGHT ABOUT BY AI ALGORITHMS

The financial industry has become more receptive to AI technology's involvement in everyday finance and trading processes. As a result, algorithmic trading could be responsible for our next major financial crisis in the markets.

While AI algorithms aren't clouded by human judgment or emotions, they also don't take into account contexts, the interconnectedness of markets and factors like human trust and fear. These algorithms then make thousands of trades at a blistering pace with the goal of selling a few seconds later for small profits. Selling off thousands of trades could scare investors into doing the same thing, leading to sudden crashes and extreme market volatility.

Instances like the 2010 Flash Crash and the Knight Capital Flash Crash serve as reminders of what could happen when trade-happy algorithms go berserk, regardless of whether rapid and massive trading is intentional.

This isn't to say that AI has nothing to offer to the finance world. In fact, AI algorithms can help investors make smarter and more informed decisions on the market. But finance organizations need to make sure they understand their AI algorithms and how those algorithms make decisions. Companies should consider whether AI raises or lowers their confidence before introducing the technology to avoid stoking fears among investors and creating financial chaos.

11. LOSS OF HUMAN INFLUENCE

An overreliance on AI technology could result in the loss of human influence — and a lack in human functioning — in some parts of society. Using AI in healthcare could result in reduced human empathy and reasoning, for instance. And applying generative AI for creative endeavors could diminish human creativity and emotional expression. Interacting with AI systems too much could even cause reduced peer communication and social skills. So while AI can be very helpful for automating daily tasks, some question if it might hold back overall human intelligence, abilities and need for community.

12. UNCONTROLLABLE SELF-AWARE AI

There also comes a worry that AI will progress in intelligence so rapidly that it will become sentient, and act beyond humans' control — possibly in a malicious manner. Alleged reports of this sentience have already been occurring, with one popular account being from a former Google engineer who stated the AI chatbot LaMDA was sentient and speaking to him just as a person would. As AI's next big milestones involve making systems with artificial general intelligence, and eventually artificial superintelligence, cries to completely stop these developments continue to rise.

How to Mitigate the Risks of AI

AI still has numerous benefits, like organizing health data and powering self-driving cars. To get the most out of this promising technology, though, some argue that plenty of regulation is necessary.

"There's a serious danger that we'll get [AI systems] smarter than us fairly soon and that these things might get bad motives and take control," Hinton told NPR. "This isn't just a science fiction problem. This is a serious problem that's probably going to arrive fairly soon, and politicians need to be thinking about what to do about it now."

DEVELOP LEGAL REGULATIONS

AI regulation has been a main focus for dozens of countries, and now the U.S. and European Union are creating more clear-cut measures to manage the rising sophistication of artificial intelligence. (In fact, President Joe Biden issued an executive order in 2023 requiring federal agencies to develop new rules and guidelines for AI safety and security.) Although this means certain AI technologies could eventually be banned, it doesn't prevent societies from exploring the field.

CREATE ORGANIZATIONAL AI STANDARDS

Preserving a spirit of experimentation is vital for Ford, who believes AI is essential for countries looking to innovate and keep up with the rest of the world.

"You regulate the way AI is used, but you don't hold back progress in basic technology. I think that would be wrong-headed and potentially dangerous," Ford said. "We decide where we want AI and where we don't; where it's acceptable and where it's not. And different countries are going to make different choices."

MAKE AI PART OF COMPANY CULTURE AND DISCUSSIONS

The key is deciding how to apply AI in an ethical manner. On a company level, there are many steps businesses can take when integrating AI into their operations. Organizations can develop processes for monitoring algorithms, compiling high-quality data and explaining the findings of AI algorithms. Leaders could even make AI a part of their company culture, establishing standards to determine acceptable AI technologies.

GUIDE TECH WITH HUMANITIES PERSPECTIVES

Though when it comes to society as a whole, there should be a greater push for tech to embrace the diverse perspectives of the humanities. Stanford University AI researchers Fei-Fei Li and John Etchemendy make this argument in a 2019 blog post that calls for national and global leadership in regulating artificial intelligence:

"The creators of AI must seek the insights, experiences and concerns of people across ethnicities, genders, cultures and socio-economic groups, as well as those from other fields, such as economics, law, medicine, philosophy, history, sociology, communications, human-computer-interaction, psychology, and Science and Technology Studies (STS)."

Balancing high-tech innovation with human-centered thinking is an ideal method for producing responsible AI technology and ensuring the future of AI remains hopeful for the next generation. The dangers of artificial intelligence should always be a topic of discussion, so leaders can figure out ways to wield the technology for noble purposes.

“I think we can talk about all these risks, and they're very real,” Ford said. “But AI is also going to be the most important tool in our toolbox for solving the biggest challenges we face.”

CONCLUSION

Artificial intelligence has the potential to transform all organizations. The process by which this transformation happens can vary, but the steps will tend to follow the roadmap we have listed in this book. Following all the steps outlined in the previous chapters will enable your organization to implement and excel in the use of AI technology. AI holds the key to unlocking a magnificent future where, driven by data and computers that understand our world, we will all make more informed decisions. These computers of the future will understand not just how to turn on the switches but why the switches need to be turned on. Even further, they may one day ask us if we need switches at all.

Although AI cannot solve all your organization's problems, it has the potential to completely change how business is done. It affects every sector, from manufacturing to finance, bringing about never before seen increases in efficiency. As more industries adopt and start experimenting with this technology, newer applications will be invented. AI will bring a change even more widespread and sweeping than the introduction of computing devices. It will change the way we transact, get diagnosed, perform surgeries, and drive our cars. It is already changing industrial processes, medical imaging, financial modeling, and computer vision. We are well on our way to tapping into this enormous potential, and as a result, the future holds better decision-making potential and faster.